Meandering Tea R

Chapte

CW01431126

(1) **Holne 4miles   Holne Tea Roo**

(2) **Lustleigh   5.5 miles   Primrose Tea Room**

(3) **Buckland in the Moor 3 miles The Wheel: Bonus Walk**

(4) **Widecombe in the Moor 3.5 miles   Wayside Café**

(5) **Buckfastleigh via Buckfast Abbey 2.5 miles The Grange**

(6) **Kingsteignton 2 miles Sampson's Farm Café**

(7) **Shaldon 5 miles The Coffee Rush Café**

(8) **Cockington 3 miles Weavers Tea Room**

(9) **Ottery St Mary 3 miles Seasons Tea Room**

(10) **Chagford   3.5 miles Victoria Sponge Tea Room**

(11) **Dartington 2.5 miles The Venus Cafe**

DISCLAIMER

The contents of the Kindle e Book are correct at time of publication. However we cannot be held responsible for any errors or omissions or changes in details or for any consequences of any reliance on the information provided. We have tried to be accurate in the book, but things can change and would be grateful if readers advise us of any inaccuracies they may encounter.

We have taken every care to ensure the walks are safe and achievable by walkers with a reasonable level of fitness. But with outdoor activities there is always a degree of risk involved and the publisher accepts no responsibility for any injury caused to readers while following these walks.

SAFETY FIRST

All the walks have been covered to ensure minimum risk to walkers that follow the routes.

Always be particularly careful if crossing main roads, but remember traffic can also be dangerous even on minor country lanes.

If in the country and around farms be careful of farm machinery and livestock (take care to put dog on lead) and observe the **Country Code**.

Also ensure you wear suitable clothing and footwear, I would advise wearing walking boots which protect from wet feet and add extra ankle support over uneven terrain.

There are a few rules that should be observed if walking alone advise somebody were you are walking and approximate time you will return. Allow plenty of time for the walk especially if it is further and or more difficult than you have walked before. Whatever the distance make sure you have enough daylight hours to complete the walk safely. When walking along a country road always walk on the right to face oncoming traffic, the only exception is on a blind bend were you cross to the left to have a clear view and can be seen from both directions.

If bad weather should come in making visibility difficult, do not panic just try to remember any features along route and get out the map to pinpoint the area but be sure before you move off, that you are moving in the right direction.

Unfortunately accidents can still happen even on the easiest of walks, if this is the case make sure the person in trouble is safe before seeking help. If carrying a mobile phone dial 999 or 112 European Union emergency number will connect you to any network to get you help.

Unmapped walks we recommend that you take the relevant Ordnance Survey map and compass with you, even if you have a Smartphone, digi-walker or G.P.S all of which can fail on route.

Introduction

The day I started out on Meandering Tea Room Walks in Devon I was very excited about all the nice Tea Rooms tucked away in the villages and hamlets spread across Devon. But I soon found that it was difficult to find this national treasure which when I was young seem to be around every corner. The hard economic times seem to put pay to a lot of the finest Tea Rooms.

But after much searching and several extra walks I came up with 11 circular walks between 2 miles and 5.5 miles. This does include one bonus walk at the Buckland Beacon which does not have a Tea Room anymore but there are several at nearby Ashburton. The reason for keeping this walk in the book is because it is so good, with the Ten Commandment's carved in the stone at Buckland Beacon and the terrain is very enjoyable for the whole family.

The terrain on the walks varies from open fields, green lanes, woodland and country lanes, with many of these areas having some great views along the way. The Tea Rooms are some of the finest in the Southwest which all add their own special piece of magic, with their cream teas and views or there nice gardens and pleasant surroundings. A lot of the Tea Rooms now also cater for good dogs.

Please remember if you have a dog to follow the Country Code keep on a lead in the lambing season and also when the birds are nesting especially around ground nesting birds to prevent birds deserting there nest and leaving the chicks to predators.

Please make sure you follow the Countryside Code, gates are normally shut by the farmers to keep farm animals in, but sometimes they may be left open so the animals can reach food or water. So be sure to leave gates as you find them or follow instructions on signs.

If you think a sign is illegal or misleading such as a PRIVATE or NO ENTRY on a public footpath then contact the local authority.

When out and about always be sure to use gates, gaps or stiles in the field boundaries if possible because climbing over walls, hedges and fences can damage them and increase the risk of farm animals escaping.

Be careful not to disturb ruins and historic sites because our heritage is for the future not just for the past.

The dog is man's best friend and is very important to a lot of us, but they too have rules. Remember to ensure dogs do not disturb wildlife, farm animals, horses or even other people keep them under effective control.

There can be special dog rules which apply in particular situations, dogs maybe banned from certain areas that people use.

The access rights that normally apply to open country know as Open Access Land require dogs to be kept on a short lead between 1st March and 31st July to help protect ground nesting birds and all year round near farm animals.

If however cattle or horses chase you and your dog it is safer to let your dog off the lead. The dog will be much safer if you let it run away from a farm animal in these circumstances and so will you.

Dog mess is unpleasant and it can cause infections, so always clean up after your dog and get rid of the mess responsibly. Make sure your dog is wormed regularly to protect it, other animals and people.

BEWARE Ticks give you Lyme disease a bacterial infection that can be passed to humans through this small blood sucking insect. Ticks can be found commonly in woodland, grassland and heathland, both here and abroad. For symptoms check the Natural England website.

Hope you all enjoy the walks which are designed to be easy to follow and all form a complete circle. Please do not forget your map as advised for each walk, the Smartphone and G.P.S can sometimes not work so a paper map and compass are a most.

Happy Walking to you all.

Meandering Tea Room Walks in Devon

Chapter 1   Holne   Tea Room and Community Shop

Park & Start; Grid ref;   SX 711709   Post Code;   TQ13 7RS

Distance: 4 miles

Level; Easy

Time: 2 hours

Terrain: There are country lanes, green lanes and open fields. Part of the track is along the Two Moors Way which runs from Ivybridge to Lynton and Lynmouth in North Devon.

Maps O.S Explorer OL 28 Dartmoor

Refreshments: Holne Tea Room and Community Shop.

River Dart.

Holne Tea Room and Community Shop

This is a very welcome sight after a long walk, a Tea Room with teas and coffee, light lunches and homemade cakes which includes the magnificent cream teas. Also check out the Community Shop for all sorts of delights.

Opening Times

11.00 am to 17.00 pm every day.

Access to start

Take the A38 Exeter to Plymouth dual carriageway and at Ashburton take slip road onto B3352, keep right at Peartree Cross. Follow lane onto Stoney Post Cross keep right and follow signs to Holne. Then at top of hill with turning to Holne off to the left, drop downhill to the bottom and cross New Bridge and park in car park on left.

The Walk

(1)

The walk starts at New Bridge car park. Exit car park and turn right over the bridge and walk past the cattle grid then on in the direction of the white house straight ahead. Just past the house turn immediately to the right up a few steps and over a stile. Cross stile and keep over to the hedge on the left slowly climb uphill then midway go through gap in hedge in the centre of field into another field and continue to the top of hill heading for a stile set back on the left in the hedge. At the stile look back over the magnificent views back down in the valley. Cross stile and follow the narrow pathway which is very uneven in places to reach a lane after about 25 metres.

(2)

Turn right on lane and walk past Chase Gate Farm on the left, then on up to the next road junction which is Stoney Post, go straight ahead at junction on uphill past the woods to the next road junction at the top of the hill with the unusual name of Gallant le Bower. Turn right here in the direction of Holne, and continue along lane for about another half mile to reach a road junction on the right with two gates opposite on left, go through the second gate to follow the wide track as you climb up over Green Down with its gorse bushes on both sides of the track. Stay on the track all the way to the end where the path narrows before reaching a gate. Go through gate to leave the Down on to an enclosed track, follow track all the way down to the end to reach a lane, and then to arrive at Ridgey Cross road junction. Keep over to the left at road junction and head off downhill in the direction of Buckfastleigh, continue to follow the lane around to the right after about 500 metres ignoring the road junction off to the left and continue to descend downhill rapidly.

(3)

Then just before a house on the right near the bottom of the hill turn right onto a track next to a small stream. Keep on track for about 25 metres before turning left through a gate marked public footpath. This then takes you through a back garden area to another gate, go through gate and rise up a grassy track to a large gate at the end. Go through gate and turn right onto a wide stoney track that starts to climb steeply up hill, this part of the walk is on the Two Moors Way.

(4)

Then just continue uphill along track to the end to reach a lane, keep over to the right then straight ahead to see the Holne boundary marker ahead then go right at this point to walk down into the village to the excellent and welcome Holne Tea Room and Community Shop. After a visit to the Tea Room continue down the slope past the church and the pub Church House Inn to reach a cross roads. Go straight across road up a slope and continue on a short distance to the end to reach a road junction, Turn left at the road junction then after just 25 metres turn right onto a narrow path marked public footpath to New Bridge. Then just follow path and the yellow way markers down the hill through fields and finally back into Holne Woods high above the River Dart which enters National Trust land, the path twist and turns following the river to reach a gate at the end. Go through gate onto road and turn left to cross over New Bridge back to the car park.

Chapter 2 Lustleigh   Primrose Tea Room

Park & Start; Grid ref;   SX 711709   Post Code; TQ13 9TJ

Distance: 5.5 miles

Level;   Moderate

Time: 2 hours 30 minutes

Terrain: This covers woodland paths and a steep climb uphill through open moorland to Hunter Tor. Then down green lanes and quiet country lanes and back through more wooded areas.

Maps O.S Explorer OL28 Dartmoor

Refreshments: Primrose Tea Room.

Track up towards Lustleigh Cleave.

Primrose Tea Room

This is a beautiful Tea Room tucked away on the edge of Dartmoor in Wrey Valley.

The food is magnificent with Victoria Sponge, Lemon Drizzle cake and Death by Chocolate. Then you have of course the Devon Cream Tea and a selection of several different jams. The speciality of the Tea Room as to be the wide selection of leaf tea, so please try something different from the tea range.

Opening Times

Friday 10.30 am to 5.00 pm
Saturday 10.30am to 5.00 pm
Sunday 11.00 am to 5.00 pm

Access to start

Go on the A38 Exeter to Plymouth dual carriageway and take the turn off onto the A382 signposted Newton Abbot, Bovey Tracey and Moretonhampstead. Then stay in right lane to exit at 4th junction through traffic lights at Heathfield, continue on A382 for about 5 miles before reaching the Lustleigh turn off on the left.

The Walk

(1)

The walk starts in the centre of Lustleigh parking where ever you can find a space. Leave the village via the road uphill with the church on your right and head uphill to the road junction turn left at this point. Then after only a few metres turn left again next to the Old School House then only to turn left again along lane marked unsuitable for heavy vehicles and signposted to the Cleave. Continue to follow lane to the end past the last house into a narrow path up to a small gate. Go through gate and then go straight ahead to reach a junction of pathways and gate, carry straight on to a kissing gate to enter into a wooded area. Once through gate follow the enclosed pathway to the end to emerge out onto a surfaced road next to a house.

(2)

Turn left past the house in the direction of the signpost marked Hammerslake for the Cleave, then off the road take a path slightly to the right between house and garages, marked with a yellow marker down the path before crossing a stream. The pathway now starts to rise quite steeply up through the woodland, up over large boulders covered in moss so please take care they can be very slippery when wet. Continue to follow the well-defined path although through the woodland to the top of hill to reach a stile. Go over stile out onto lane, turn left and after about 25 metres turn right up a bridleway marked Lustleigh Cleave. The track slowly rises now up to a gate, go through gate and then straight ahead with the signpost indicating Hunters Tor. Stay on this path as it rises up steeply in parts through the woods along a clearly defined path on past the Donkeys Cave and on to the top of the hill. Then as you start to emerge out of the woods near to Sharpitor be sure to look at the views down the Wrey Valley and the open moorland on the far side of the valley.

(3)

Turn right at this point and then follow the ridge through a wooded area, which then turns into open moorland with the path winding through gorse and boulders still rising up hill for over a mile in the direction of Hunters Tor, but take time to look out at the views over many villages nestling in the valley. Just before you reach Hunters Tor you will see the banks and ditches of an Old Iron Age Fort with views out over Haytor and Hound Tor and many more on a clear day. Follow path around the back of the Fort to a gate set back in the wall just before Hunters Tor. Go through gate marked with a sign that says Path, then follow track all the way downhill to the bottom, which then reaches a wider track, then keep over to the right still on the track to walk past Peck Farm on right. Once past farm head for large gate straight ahead near some out buildings, go through gate and turn left down a track which you follow for about 100 metres then at the bend in the road turn left to go through gateway signposted Foxworthy Bridge.

(4)

Follow the track along the Bovey Valley for about a mile with a beautiful ancient stone wall on the left for quite a distance to finally reach a gate. Go through gate to pass the beautiful Foxworthy Cottage on the left then veer right down slope and after just a few metres turn left signposted to Hammerslake, just down from the signpost is Foxworthy Bridge which you may like to view on a slight detour. To continue walk follow track onto the right then past the entrance to the Old Foxworthy Mill then go left and follow the signpost to a gate. Go through gate and continue to follow path through the woodland twisting in all directions. Then at the next signpost go straight on to start a very long climb uphill through the woods. At the next junction keep left near some large boulders and soon after at next sign turn right and follow path for about a mile still rising to reach a clump of large boulders on left at a junction of paths. The signpost is marked Hammerslake so at this point turn left.

(5)

Once having turned left onto the track this then continues to climb up hill then at the top you drop downhill finally reaching the gate you entered on the outward journey. Go through gate to reach lane and turn right, follow lane to next road junction and turn down left to descend downhill passing Ellimore Farm and continue on lane and downhill to the bottom. After passing houses along the way you reach a woodland with a wide track off to the left signpost Path this then goes into the woods and across a stream, once in woods turn immediately to the right just before a gate and follow path along to the stream which you re-cross via large boulders which are used as a bridge (be careful you do not slip). Follow path back into woodland to reach a network of paths and then turn left and head for a gate, go through gate and over bridge into a community grassy area with a playground and follow through to the end and exit via a gate to emerge by the Post Office in the centre of Lustleigh opposite the church.

Park & Start; Grid ref;   SX 738738   Post Code; TQ13 7DX tea rooms in Ashburton.

Distance: 3.5 miles

Level; Moderate

Time: 1 hour 45 minutes

Terrain: Two steep climbs and quiet country lanes, green lanes and some rough moorland with a steep descend through gorse wooded area and bracken.

Maps: O.S Explorer OL28 Dartmoor

Refreshments: See under Ashburton.

Buckland in the Moor.

Wheel Café once part of Round House Craft Centre.

Much to my dismay this great craft centre and tea room is no more, so for tea you will have to travel a couple of miles back into Ashburton.

Check out the Studio Teashop Ashburton, this is well worth the detour. Great food with homemade cake selection, morning coffee, lunch time meals and Devon Cream Tea.

Opening Times

Monday to Saturday 9.30 am to 5.00 pm

Closed Wednesday.

Access to start

Go on the Exeter to Plymouth A38 dual carriageway and exit slip road onto the B3352. Turn right at Peartree Cross still on the B3352, then bear left on road before turn turning right to Hele Cross, go straight ahead at Hele Cross. Then continue straight onto Water Turn onto Buckland in the Moor, before reaching Buckland turn right to Widecombe and follow road for mile over cattle grid and park on either side of road, this is just before Cold East Cross.

The Walk

(1)

The walk starts at the informal car parking area just past the cattle grid and before Cold East Cross. **N.B.** There is a car park further on down the road near Cold East Cross if necessary. Cross road at parking area and keep to the left of wall, follow the stone wall uphill heading in the direction of Buckland Beacon straight ahead then at top go through gate on right. Once at Buckland Beacon check out the views all around and take a look at the Ten Commandments carved in the stone. Then continue to follow the path with the wall on your left downhill this then starts to descend very steeply as it twist through brambles and gorse and is not very well-defined in places. Then after going past several trees you will finally reach a gate, go through the gate into a short section of woodland before emerging out over a gap in the hedge onto a lane.

(2)

Turn right on lane then follow for about half mile to reach what was once the Old Round House Craft Centre and the Wheel Café **N.B.(There is now no Tea Room but I thought the walk is so good I just had to include it because refreshments are available at nearby Ashburton).** So continue the walk along the road through the quaint hamlet of Buckland in the Moor with its magnificent thatched cottages and stream that runs past the cottages away on your right. The road then starts to rise uphill to the church. Just past the church turn right up Elliot's Hill a tarmac no through road. Continue to follow the road as it steadily rises up the hill and past Elliot's Hill Farm on the right. Then after about 300 metres past the farm turn right down a lane follow all the way to the bottom of slope to Bowden's Farm on the right. Then veer away to the left onto a track over a bridge across a stream and then through a large gate. This takes you on an old sunken track next to a wooded area on left then just continue uphill for about half mile to reach a gate at the top.

(3)

Once through the gate you are now back on Buckland Common, Follow track uphill to the right which brings you back to the wall you followed on the outward journey, then from here turn left downhill and retrace your steps back to the car.

Chapter 4 Widecombe in the Moor   Wayside Café

Park & Start; Grid ref;   SX 738738   Post Code; TQ13 7TA

Distance: 3.5 miles

Level; Easy

Time: 1 hour 30 minutes

Terrain: Mostly quiet country lanes through open moorland, with one very steep climb at the start.

Maps: O.S Explorer OL 28 Dartmoor

Refreshments: Wayside Café.

Widecombe in the Moor.

Wayside Café

This is a magnificent café in the very heart of Dartmoor, with its quaint green and pretty church and the Dartmoor ponies all roaming free.

The Wayside Café menu is very complete from Cream Teas, light bites or Sunday Roast for visitors or hungry walkers it is all available.

Opening Times

Saturdays to Thursday 10.30 am to 4.30 pm
Closed Fridays
N.B Opening can be affected by the weather in this area.

Access to start

Take the A38 Exeter to Plymouth dual carriageway then at slip road to Newton Abbot/ Bovey Tracey and exit 4th turn onto A382 into Bovey Tracey at next roundabout take 2nd exit and then finally at the next exit take 1st exit onto B3387 and follow signs to Widecombe in the Moor.

The Walk

(1)

The walk starts at the green in the centre of Widecombe, and then take the road that goes past the church on the right then you drop down a slope to pass by what was the Old Post Office on your right and the primary school. Then continue along the road for just over half mile looking back at the views around Widecombe. Turn right at the first junction at Southcombe Cross and start to climb up a very steep hill past what forms a crossroads with a track either side of the road at this point you are on the open moor, stay on the road to the top of the hill. Then you drop downhill dramatically to reach a crossroads at the bottom of the hill, turn left and walk along a level road listen to the sounds which are very clear along this stretch of road with the cuckoo, sheep bleating, cows and in the distance peacocks calling, but best of all no traffic noise. Continue on the lane for about a mile and when the lane then starts to go down a slope to reach Jordan Cross keep over to the left and continue to follow the lane downhill.

(2)

Then after going downhill for about another half mile you reach the next junction East Lane Cross, turn left and follow the sign marked Widecombe continue to follow this lane for nearly a mile as it twist and winds it way back past the Widecombe boundary sign and on back into the centre of the village.

Chapter 5 Buckfastleigh via Buckfast Abbey: The Grange

Park & Start; Grid ref;   SX 741661   Post Code; TQ11 0EE

Distance: 2.5 miles

Level; Easy

Time: 1 hour 30 minutes

Terrain: Narrow paths, open fields and quiet country lanes.

Maps: O.S. Explorer OL 28 Dartmoor

Refreshments: The Grange.

Buckfast Abbey.

The Grange

The Grange is set in a beautiful position in the Buckfast Abbey grounds, with great views of the Abbey and surrounding area.

The food is very good with a large range of homemade cakes, croissants and pastries baked fresh every morning. There is also a good selection of teas, cold drinks and coffee. Then there is the light snacks, homemade soups and sandwiches. Do not forget to make room for your Devon Cream Tea.

Opening Times

Monday to Saturday 10.00 am to 5.00 pm (winter close 4.00 pm).
Sundays 10.00 am to 4.30 pm.

Access to start
Take the A38 Exeter to Plymouth dual carriageway and exit slip road to Buckfastleigh. Turn right onto A384 which changes to B3380, then go right onto Elliot Plain, the road changes name to Fore Street. Then at end turn right onto Station Road for car park.

The Walk

(1)

The walk starts in the car park at Station Road, exit car park and turn right across bridge and then cross road to climb steps up to the left, go to the top of steps and then go through a gate. Continue to follow the narrow pathway to the end which joins a surfaced road, turn left and go past the ruins of the old parish church which is now being refurbished. Stay on this lane passing Churchill Farm on your left before reaching a triangular road junction, keep over to the right and then almost immediately turn right again to go through a kissing gate. Follow the well-defined path through the top of the field keeping to hedge on left, then at the end of the field go through another kissing gate to drop down a narrow path, then after few 100 metres you go through yet another kissing gate where you get your first view of Buckfast Abbey in the distance.

(2)

Continue on down the track as it widens towards the bottom before reaching the main road, turn left at road and go past Buckfast Post Office on your right and then bearing over to your right go under the arch to enter the Abbey grounds. The Grange Tea Room is straight down the path with Buckfast Abbey off to the right. To continue your walk after tea retrace your route back to the top of the hill to the triangular road junction and turn right down Church Hill a no through road and follow all the way to the bottom where it narrows down to a pathway. Follow path to the end which comes out on to Holne Road and turn left, then after only about 50 metres turn right down Church Street passing the Sun Inn stay straight ahead as the road changes to Bridge Street and still carry straight on it then goes into Market Street. At the end veer around to the left onto Chapel Street and on past the Catholic Church on the left, still follow the road to reach the main street through Buckfastleigh keep over to the left to enter Station Road to return to the car park.

Chapter 6 Kingsteignton Sampson's Farm Café

Park & Start; Grid ref;   SX 741661   Post Code; TQ12 3PP

Distance: 2 miles

Level; Easy

Time: 1 hour

Terrain: Open fields and through wooded area along uneven paths

Maps: O.S Explorer 110 Torquay and Dawlish

Refreshments: Sampson's Farm Café

River Teign.

Sampson's Farm Cafe

This is a beautiful 15th century thatched hotel set in the hamlet of Preston just outside of Kingsteignton.

The food is very good but I am not sure whether they now serve just coffee and cream teas, it seems to have moved more to being Sampson's Farm Country Hotel with self-catering, and restaurant?

Access to start

Exeter to Torquay on the A380 and exit slip road into Kingsteignton, go past the Ten Tor Inn and at new road junction go right to Chudleigh at next roundabout take first exit and follow lane to traffic lights, go straight ahead and over Teignbridge to take first turning left into car park.

The Walk

(1)

The walk starts at the car park next to Teignbridge along the old road to Teigngrace. Exit car park and cross road carefully to go through gate right opposite. Then follow the well-defined footpath along the River Teign for almost a mile through three fields before reaching a bridge on right with a signpost indicating the Templar Way along the River Teign. Cross over bridge up the slope and turn left for Sampson's Farm along an uneven track for 50 metres to reach the Farm on the right.

(2)

Then after refreshments retreat back down the track to the bridge and carry straight on past the bridge up the slope to a gate. Go through the gate and then follow the clear pathway through the wooded area and open fields again along the River Teign for almost a mile to finally reach the road. Turn right on the road and take care as you cross the Teignbridge, cross road and return to the car park.

Chapter 7 Shaldon via Stokeinteignhead and Ringsmore Café Rush

Park & Start; Grid ref;   SX 938717   Post Code; TQ14 0DE

Distance: 5 miles

Level; Strenuous

Time: 2hours 30 minutes

Terrain: Southwest Coast Path, green lanes, country lanes and roads through villages with some very steep climbs with the odd muddy section.

Maps: O.S Explorer 110 Torquay and Dawlish

Refreshments: The Coffee Rush Café.

The view out towards Shaldon Bridge.

The Coffee Rush Café

Coffee Rush is a splendid café along the walk, set back in Shaldon on Fore Street. In 2011 it was named in The Times has being in the 30 best places for tea, and for three years in a row it was the finalist in the Devon Life's Coffee and Tearoom of the Year.

The food is very good with cream teas and light snacks along with a good selection of tea and coffee.

Opening Times

Monday to Saturday 8.00 am to 5.00 pm
Sunday   9.00 am to 5.00 pm
Bank Holidays   10.00 am to 5.00 pm

Dog Friendly.

Access to start
Exeter to Torquay A380 and exit slip road to Teignmouth, at second lot of traffic lights turn right over Shaldon Bridge and follow road towards Torquay, climb hill out Shaldon area and at top turn left marked The Ness and Zoo and follow down to car park.

The Walk

(1)

The walk starts in the upper Ness car park. Exit car park in top left corner onto an uneven track which forms part of the Southwest Coast Path, the first lot of steps on the left lead up to a viewing platform. To continue the walk stay on the track to the next lot of steps on left this then takes you up through a woodland positioned down at the bottom end of the golf course. Go through a gate which continues along a grassy path which then starts to climb uphill very steeply, finally reaching the main road at the top where you then go through a gate just before road.

(2)

Turn left once through gate then after only a few metres go back on a narrow path which is marked on the left Coast Path and follow for a short distance before re-emerging back on a pavement next to the main road. Then walk to the end of the pavement and past a driveway on the left before turning left on another narrow path marked Coast Path to Maidencombe. Continue to follow path up hill and down dale before arriving in the car park overlooking Labrador Bay. Go straight through the car park to the far end to a gate, then once in field just follow the well-defined path to another gate. Again go through gate into a field and continue on downhill to the bottom to a gate positioned on the right setback in the hedge. Go through gate and then carefully cross the main road to the opposite side of road, then at the end of the layby go off to the right onto a green lane and continue to follow lane to the top of the hill.

(3)

Then at the top of the hill the main track veers off to the left, at this point take the green lane on the right and follow for about a mile all the way into Stokeinteignhead. Then at the end of the green lane it comes out onto a road, turn left and after only a few metres you reach a road junction with the Church House Inn straight ahead. Turn right onto the main road through the village and after a few metres take the next junction off to the right onto Forches Hill. Continue to climb uphill almost to the top and on reaching the Stokeinteignhead boundary sign turn left onto another green lane (part of this section can be muddy depending on the weather) but stay on this track for about a mile and take time to soak up the views out over the Teign Estuary to Shaldon Bridge before reaching the Newton Abbot to Shaldon Road. Turn right on the road and go past several holiday camps on into Ringsmore and continue to follow the road back into Shaldon. Once at the main road to Torquay turn slightly left at junction and then cross the pedestrian crossing and enter the main street at Shaldon go past the Coffee Rush Café or stop for refreshments, then carry on past the pedestrian ferry and continue on through Marine Parade, before rising uphill to the Ness House Hotel. Go past the hotel bearing around to path on the left then walk back uphill to the car park.

Chapter 8 Cockington Weavers Cottage Tea Room

Park & Start; Grid ref;   SX 893638   Post Code; TQ 2 6XA

Distance: 3 miles

Level; Easy

Time: 1 hour 30 minutes

Terrain: Through Cockington Country Park, woodlands and open fields with a small section on country lanes.

Maps: O.S Explorer 110 Torquay and Dawlish.

Refreshments: Weavers Cottage Tea Room.

Gamekeepers Cottage Cockington Country Park.

The Weavers Tea Room

This is an amazing Tea Room set in an 18th century cottage with a delightful walled courtyard garden near the Cockington Country Park entrance.

The food is very good which feature light lunches, the speciality is Devon Cream Teas or there is homemade cake. There is also a great selection of tea and coffee with very good service. Be sure to try the Cheese Ploughman's one of the best I have had anywhere.

Opening Times

Monday to Saturday 9.00 am to 5.00 pm.
Sunday 10.00 am to 4.00 pm

Dog Friendly

Access to start

Exeter to Torquay A380 into Torquay head for the sea front, just near the hotels look for turning off to Cockington signposted very clearly.

The Walk

(1)

The walk starts in the car park in the centre of Cockington. Exit car park and turn left, cross road carefully and veer around the bend keeping over to the right passing between the Smithy and Weavers Cottage Tea Room. Follow the lane for about 25 metres and then turn right at the Cockington Country Park sign up to the gate and then enter the park. Once in the park take the track off to the left signposted to the Gamekeepers Cottage, go under the bridge which supports the Totnes Road and then after 30 metres take the path to the right to the Gamekeepers Cottage straight ahead just in front of Manacombe Woods.

(2)

Then once at the cottage follow the path off to the right through Manacombe Woods for about half a mile to emerge just in front of the Warren Barn. At this point there is a criss cross of paths, but turn left up the wide bridleway or along the narrow footpath next to the edge of a field, both leading to the top of hill at the same junction signposted Scadson Wood. Turn right at the top of hill and follow path down into Scadson Wood and continue to follow the new pathway for about a mile, then with the Mountain Bike Trail on the right stay on path keeping over to the left up a steep short climb, then midway up sweep around to the right.

(3)

Continue to stay on the new pathway for about half a mile, the new track continues on uphill and at the top you will reach Occombe Park. But do not go uphill cross the bridge over the stream onto the old track into the old car park now closed off to vehicles. Exit the car park onto the lane and turn right, climb uphill to the top and with a driveway on the right take the entrance through the gate on the opposite side of road through a large metal gate. This is a public footpath the sign is high up on the telegraph pole which cannot be seen from the road. Follow the track through the field into the farmyard through the gate and cross the farmyard to another gate following the yellow waymark signs. Once through the second gate turn right after 25 metres down track between farm buildings past the farm house on the right. At the bottom of track it veers off to the left, but go straight ahead through a gate into a field, keep on track uphill to the top of the field and through a gateway, still on the well-defined track through the next field to reach two gates straight ahead at the end.

(4)

Go through gate on the left and follow the narrow path next to the hedge on right (sometimes overgrown in places) down to a stile, cross the stile and follow the well maintained new pathway straight on through the countryside ignoring any junctions to finally reach a road. Turn right on road past the Alms-house's on the left and then past the Drum Inn on the right to reach the car park just a bit further down on the left.

Chapter 9 Ottery St Mary Seasons Tea Room

Park & Start; Grid ref; SY 095955   Post Code; EX11 1DB

Distance: 3 miles

Level; Easy

Time: 1 hour 30 minutes

Terrain: Open meadows, country lanes and riverbank paths through woodland, this can be muddy in wet weather and uneven under foot.

Maps: O.S. Explorer 115 Exmouth and Sidmouth

Refreshments: Seasons Tea Room.

River Otter.

Seasons Tea Room

The Seasons Tea Room is a classic old-fashioned beautiful teashop, with its lace tablecloths and cake trolley.

The food is great Devon Cream Teas, lemon sponge cake, chocolate cake and meringues. But if it is lunch you are looking for then there is a selection of soups and salads, or maybe West Country Rarebit made from cheddar cheese and cider served with a poached egg on top.

Also out the back is a very nice garden which is dog friendly, with table and chairs nicely positioned throughout the garden areas?

Opening Times
Monday to Saturday 9.00 am to 5.00 pm
Leave car park in Ottery and walk past Sainsbury's on your left on Hind Street, turn left into Sadler Lane and go the end. Turn left onto Gold Street and after a few metres turn left again onto Silver Street.

Access to start
Leave M5 at junction 29 off slip road onto A30. Follow A30 to Daisymount and exit slip road to follow road into Ottery St Mary.

The Walk

(1)

The walk starts in the car park off Canaan Way. Exit car park and turn left along road past the water leat then on past Dunkirk Cottages on the right. Carry straight on and at Cadhay Bridge Farm then turn left and continue onto Cadhay Bridge, cross the bridge over the River Otter then follow lane over the Talewater Bridge across the small River Tale, then on over the old railway crossing with the old crossing gates still embedded in the hedge next to the crossing keeper's cottage.

(2)

Then continue on lane and through a gateway on the left you will catch a glimpse of Cadhay House, then just before you reach the driveway to the house cross the road and turn right at a public footpath sign next to a stile. Cross the stile and follow the defined footpath through a meadow and then cross over a small bridge across the River Tale. Once over the bridge head diagonally slightly to the right in the direction of a small gate in opposite corner set back in the hedge. Go through the gate and keep to the right in the next field to reach an open gateway at the end next to a cottage, this then leads onto a short track before reaching the road. Turn right at road which takes you past Taleford Farm and on into the little hamlet of Taleford. Once in Taleford you pass Gosford Park on the right where the road then starts to narrow, continue on along the lane for about another half a mile to reach a road junction at the end of the lane.

(3)

Turn right at the road junction with Gosford House directly opposite and continue to follow the lane for a further half a mile before crossing the former railway line again with yet another crossing keeper's cottage before reaching a red brick built bridge over the River Otter. Cross the bridge and after 50 metres turn right at a public footpath sign and follow the direction of the yellow markers keeping over to the left. Go through a gate and climb up the bank into a wooded area and follow path to reach a stile. Cross stile and exit wood and keep over to right along the edge of a field. Then at the end of the field there is another stile cross over and re-enter woods. Once in woods keep to the high path up above the River Otter this section can be very muddy if the weather as been wet and it is also very uneven under foot.

(4)

Continue to follow the high path for about half a mile, it twist and turns and then finally drops down then at the second footbridge turn right to cross a small stream. Then once over bridge turn left and follow the track just a short distance to reach the end, this then leads out on to the road. At this point you re-joins the outward route near Cadhay Bridge Farm, turn left and retrace your steps back into Ottery St Mary.

Chapter 10 Chagford Victoria Sponge

Park & Start; Grid ref; SX 701874   Post Code; TQ13 8AH

Distance: 3 miles

Level; Moderate

Time: 1 hour 45 minutes

Terrain: Across Nattadon Common with a very steep climb then through meadows and river paths taking in part of the Two Moors Way with another steep climb back into Chagford.

Maps: O.S Explorer OL 28 Dartmoor

Refreshments: Victoria Sponge Café.

River Teign.

Victoria Sponge Café

The Victoria Sponge Café is set in the centre of Chagford next to The Square.

The food is very good with Devon Cream Teas plus a great mug of coffee which is just what is required after a nice walk. There is also a good selection of homemade cakes to enjoy. This also is a dog friendly café so your best friend can also have a snack?

Access to start

Leave M5 at the end near Exeter and join the A30 heading to Cornwall, then stay on the A30 for 14 miles to Whiddon Down take the slip road to the left and follow signpost to Chagford.

The Walk

(1)

The walk starts at Chagford car park, exit via pathway near car entrance and walk down past Jubilee Hall to reach the road junction on High Street opposite church. Then turn left into New Street and continue to walk on past the Old School House on left, near this point the road changes into Meldon Road. Continue along Meldon Road for about 500 metres before turning left into Nattadon Road, then follow up a slope for about 60 metres, then just before the last two houses turn left up a steep slopping path signposted public footpath (Nattadon Common). Climb up the slope to a gate, go through gate and cross a stream then keep over to the left and rise steeply before veering off to the right to exit the wooded area out onto an open hillside with thick bracken.

(2)

The track is well-defined but very steep, the views at the top are worth the climb uphill. Once near to the top follow the track off to the left which runs parallel with the fence to finally reach a space that is used as a car park. Now at the top the views are out over Castle Drogo perched high on the opposite side across the Teign Gorge. Leave the car park area via the lane and turn left to cross the cattle grid, then after 25 metres turn right at gate signposted footpath to Great Weeke.

(3)

Keep over to the right on path soon to reach another gate, go through gate and turn left to continue down a path through thick grass to reach a stile at the bottom of field. Cross over stile and keep to the hedge on the left through a meadow, this continues on down the hill before entering a wooded area this then links to an ancient lane but still carry on downhill through the gorse and bracken, with the pathway still remaining well-defined to reach a gate which takes you past a sunken lane with the path descending steeply down to the road.

(4)

Turn right on road and then follow lane for a short distance to Westcott Cross a road junction signposted Adley Lane and at this point turn left. Continue along lane for about 500 metres and then turn left at a wide opening in hedge which leads you up a track to a gateway. Keep over to the right once through gateway and head diagonally across field to a stile in the bottom corner. Cross the stile into another field and again head diagonally slightly off to the right across the field to reach a stile with a (Neighbourhood Watch) sign on the fence. Go over stile and follow the narrow path through to reach a driveway, turn left on drive and follow out to main road.

(5)

Turn left on main road cross road and after 50 metres turn right down a footpath marked Rushford Bridge. Follow the narrow path as it twist and turns before reaching a paddock go through gate and cross paddock to the gate on the opposite side, again go through gate onto an enclosed pathway follow to the end to exit over a stile out onto a lane. Turn right on lane to cross Rushford Bridge, then almost immediately turn left through a gate and keeping slightly to the right head for a gateway in the hedge. Go through gateway keep around to the left to cross a footbridge then onto a stile and follow signpost to Chagford.

(6)

The route now follows the river for more than half a mile over stiles, footbridges and through gates along what is part of the Two Moors Way, which you continue to follow until reaching the road. Then turn left at the road and cross over the Old Chagford Bridge, then continue to follow lane to a crossroads, turn left at crossroads and follow lane as it rises very steeply back up in towards Chagford. Stay on lane back into the town centre and then retrace your steps back to the car park.

Chapter 11 Dartington Hall   Venus Café

Park & Start; Grid ref; SX 798628   Post Code; TQ9 6TQ

Distance: 2.5 miles

Level; Easy

Time: 1 hour 30 minutes

Terrain: country lanes and public footpaths slight uphill path through woodland.

Maps: O.S Explorer 110 Torquay and Dawlish

Refreshments: The Venus Café.

Out in the country near Dartington Hall.

The Venus Café

The Venus Café Dartington Cider Press

The food is good at the Venus Café with a menu which includes full English breakfast, burgers, vegetarian selection and seafood. There is also light snacks, salads, sandwiches and baguettes and of course cream teas.

Opening Times

Every day 8.30 am to 5.00 pm.

Access to start

Take the A30 Exeter to Plymouth dual carriageway then after about 20 miles take the slip road towards Buckfastleigh/Totnes. Turn left onto A384 towards Totnes then after 4 miles turn left next to church and follow sign post to Dartington Hall.

The Walk

(1)

The Walk starts at one of the car parks opposite Dartington Hall. Turn right out of car park and walk uphill then when you are opposite the Granary building turn right into Park Road. Continue down the road following the signpost to Warren Lane and Warren House. Once at a road junction fork off to the left still heading for Warren House following the lane to the end, with two large gates in front of you take the one on the left with a small kissing gate for pedestrians next to it and enter on to a track. Follow the track alongside the estate wall for about a half a mile or more through gates and open fields before dropping down a slope in the field to a gate at the bottom of a small fenced area, go through gate at the edge of the woods.

(2)

Do not enter the woods but after a few metres swing sharp left and exit another gate onto a hard-core track, follow this through to reach a rough concrete road which then carries on uphill for about half a mile to Old Parsonage Farm, stay on the track straight through the centre of the farm buildings to finally reach the public road.

(3)

Once at the road turn right and after just 150 metres turn left down a public footpath, follow path across the access road on into Dartington Cider Press.

(4)

Then after a short stay at the various shops and café continue on down the footpath to meet the main road and stream running parallel with the footpath. The path then leads on into a wooded area but keep over to the left as it rises uphill. When you reach two steps fork left up steps and follow path up through the woods to the top of the hill to come out on the driveway near the Foxhole Centre. Turn left on drive go through gate and drop down the road into the car park. Follow the pedestrian signs to exit car park onto a pavement. Then follow pavement on past the Totnes and Dartington Sports Field and continue to follow lane back to the end to reach a road junction.

(5)

Turn right at road junction and follow the footpath all the way back up the hill to the top. Once at the top cross the road onto the Upper Drive footpath and follow back to the car park.

Printed in Great Britain
by Amazon.co.uk, Ltd.,
Marston Gate.